DISCAR
D0844489

EX LIBRIS

SOUTH ORANGE
PUBLIC LIBRARY

SENECA'S OEDIPUS

SENECA'S
OEDIPUS

Adapted by Ted Hughes

Introduction by Peter Brook

Illustrated by Reginald Pollack

DOUBLEDAY & COMPANY, INC.,
Garden City, New York   1972

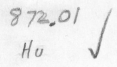

Note: SENECA'S OEDIPUS is the sole property of the author
and is fully protected by copyright. It may not be acted by
professionals or amateurs without formal permission and the
payment of a royalty. All rights, including professional,
amateur, stock, radio and television broadcasting, motion
picture, recitation, lecturing, public reading, and the rights
of translation in foreign languages are reserved. All inquiries
should be addressed to the author's agent: Olwyn Hughes,
Flat B, 10 Arkwright Road, London, N.W. 3, England.

ISBN: 0-385-00574-1 Trade
ISBN: 0-385-00662-4 Paperback
LIBRARY OF CONGRESS CATALOG CARD NUMBER 72–76172
INTRODUCTION AND ILLUSTRATIONS COPYRIGHT © 1972
        BY DOUBLEDAY & COMPANY, INC.
TEXT COPYRIGHT © 1969 BY TED HUGHES
ALL RIGHTS RESERVED
PRINTED IN THE UNITED STATES OF AMERICA
FIRST EDITION

INTRODUCTION

Seneca's play has no external action whatsoever. It may never have been acted during the author's lifetime, but possibly it was read aloud in the bathhouse to friends. Anyway, it takes place nowhere, the people are not people, and the vivid action, as it moves through the verbal images, leaps forward and back with the technique of the cinema and with a freedom beyond film.

So this is theater liberated from scenery, liberated from costume, liberated from stage moves, gestures, and business. We may not wish to observe this, but at least we know where to begin. All the play really demands is a group of actors, standing stock-still. However, this motionless actor must speak. He must set his voice in motion. To do so, many other motions must invisibly be activated in him: the still exterior must cover an extraordinary inner dynamism. Today, a body-conscious theater has liberated a generation of actors who can express a powerful emotional charge through intense physical activity. This text demands not less than that, but more: it asks physically developed actors not to go backward but to push forward on the most difficult direction—to the discovery of how leaps, rolls, and somersaults

5

can turn into acrobatics of larynx and lung. Above all, this text demands a lost art—the art of impersonal acting.

How can acting be impersonal? I can see at once what would happen if a trusting actor hearing this word and trying to be faithful to its suggestion tried to depersonalize himself: his face a set of taut muscles, his voice a foghorn, he could produce unnatural rhythms; perhaps he might believe that fashionably he was taking his place in ritual theater—but while seeming hieratic to himself he would just seem phony to us. And yet if he simply allows free rein to his personality, if he sees acting as a form of personal expression, another phonyness can easily appear, which swamps the text in a morass of groans and cries, all stemming from a ready exposure of all his own phobias and fears. The worst features of the experimental theater come from a sincerity that is essentially insincere. Such a state is at once exposed when words appear, for a false emotion clogs clarity.

Of course, all acting is made by people and so is personal. Yet it is very important to try to distinguish between the form of personal expression that is useless and self-indulgent and the sort of expression in which being impersonal and being truly individual are one and the same thing. This confusion about what of himself the actor is supposed to give is a central problem of contemporary acting—an attempt to stage this text of OEDIPUS brings it into focus.

How can the actor approach this text? One common method would be to identify himself with the characters of the play. The actor looks for psychological similarities between Oedipus and himself. If I were Oedipus, he would say, I would do X, Y, or Z because I remember

6

that when my father . . . He tries to analyze Oedipus and Jocasta as "real people" and is bound to discover the total failure of this approach. Jocasta and Oedipus may be concentrations of human meaning—but they are not personalities.

There is another approach to acting which throws psychology aside and seeks only to release the irrational in the actor's nature. He tries to cultivate a form of trance to awake his subconscious, and it is easy for him to think that he is getting closer to the level of universal myth. He can easily imagine that out of these he can draw valid dramatic material. But he must beware of being taken for a ride by a dream—the trip into the subconscious can be an illusion that feeds an illusion—and his acting remains where it was.

It is not enough for the actor to find his truth—it is not enough for him to be open blindly to impulses from sources inside himself that he cannot understand. He needs an understanding that must in turn ally itself to a wider mystery. He can only find this link through a tremendous awe and respect for what we call form. This form is the movement of the text, this form is his own individual way of capturing that movement.

It is not for nothing that the greatest of poets always have needed to work on existing material. OEDIPUS was never "invented"—before the Greek dramatists there were the legends—the Roman writer reworked the same material—Shakespeare often reworked Seneca, and now Ted Hughes reworks Seneca and through him reaches the myth. And an interesting question arises: Why in great drama is there a wish amongst creative and inventive men *not* to invent? Why do

7

they put so little store on personal invention? Is there a secret here? In serving a pre-existing pattern, it is not himself and his own meaning that the dramatist is trying to impose—it is something he is seeking to transmit. Yet to transmit properly he realizes that all of him—from his skills, his associations, to the deepest secrets of his subconscious—has to be potentially ready to leap into play, into rhythmic order, to act as carriers. The poet is a carrier, the words are carriers. So a meaning is caught in a net. Words drawn on paper are the mesh of the net. It is not for nothing that Ted Hughes, most individual of poets, is also the most concentrated. It is by his rigorous eliminating of all unnecessary decoration, all useless expressions of personality, that he gets to a form that is both his own and not his own.

So we return to the actor. Can he be a carrier too in the same way? It involves his understanding two very difficult concepts—distance and presence. Distance as Brecht has described it means keeping his personality at arm's length. It means the individual voluntarily subduing many subjective impulses, because he wishes something to appear that for him is more objective. What can help to do this? Not a moral or an artistic decision. Willful dehumanizing is mechanical—and many Brecht productions have shown how easy it is to fall into this trap—using the will power of the intellect as a sort of Pentagon holding rebel elements at bay. The only help is understanding—the more the actor understands his exact function on all levels, the more he finds the right performance pitch. To take a very simple example, a radio newsreader is intuitively impersonal and distant because he understands his function—he is a voice put at the disposal of making a

8

news sheet clear—he needs clarity and tempo—his intonations must be neither too warm nor too dry—and yet for him to bring his personal emotions to bear on the information, coloring it according to whether the news makes him bright or sad, would be silly. The actor's task is infinitely more complex than that of the newsreader. The way opens when he sees that presence is not opposed to distance. Distance is a commitment to total meaning: presence is a total commitment to the living moment: the two go together. For this reason, the most eclectic use of rehearsal exercises—to develop rhythm, listening, tempo, pitch, ensemble thinking, or critical awareness—is most valuable provided none of them is considered a method. What they can do is to increase the actor's concern—in body and in spirit—for what the play is asking. If the actor truly feels this question to be his own he is unavoidably caught in a need to share it, in a need for the audience. Out of this need for a link with an audience comes an equally strong need for absolute clarity. This is the need that eventually brings forth the means. It forges the living link with the poet's matrix, which in turn is the link with the original theme.

PETER BROOK

December 1970

SENECA'S OEDIPUS

The first performance of *Oedipus* was given at the Old Vic Theatre, London, by the National Theatre Company on March 19, 1968. The cast was as follows:

OEDIPUS	John Gielgud
JOCASTA	Irene Worth
CREON	Colin Blakely
TIRESIAS	Frank Wylie
MANTO	Louise Purnell
MESSENGER	Ronald Pickup
PHORBAS	Harry Lomax

and

Alan Adams	Bernard Gallagher	John Nightingale
Gillian Barge	Jonathan Hardy	Jeremy Rowe
David Belcher	Luke Hardy	George Selway
Helen Bourne	Roderick Horn	Terence Taplin
Patrick Carter	Gerald James	Robert Tayman
Anna Carteret	Lewis Jones	Gary Waldhorn
Kenneth Colley	Richard Kay	Benjamin Whitrow
Oliver Cotton	Jane Lapotaire	Judy Wilson
Neil Fitzpatrick	Philip Locke	Peter Winter
Roger Forbes	Kenneth Mackintosh	

Produced and designed by Peter Brook

Associate Producer: Geoffrey Reeves
Music and sound organization: Richard Peaslee
Special costumes designed by Jean Monod
Lighting by Robert Ornbo
Assistant Designer: Sue Plummer
Stage Manager: John Rothenberg

show us
show us
a simple riddle   lift everything aside

show us
a childish riddle

what has four legs at dawn
two legs at noon   three legs at dusk

and is it weakest when it has most?

"I will find the answer"   is that an answer?

show us

ACT ONE

CHORUS: night is finished   but day is reluctant   the sun
drags itself up out of that filthy cloud   it stares
down at our sick earth   it brings a gloom not light

beneath it our streets homes temples gutted with the
plague   it is one huge plague pit   the new heaps
of dead spewed up everywhere   hardening in the
sickly daylight

OEDIPUS: and I was happy   escaping from my father Polybus
freedom not exile   wandering   unafraid   a
prince   fleeing yes but unafraid   till I stumbled
as God in heaven saw me I stumbled on this kingdom

fear   that came after me   it followed me   the
fear   the words of the oracle   some day I would
kill my father   I would kill him   and worse
that other   worse   what can be worse   the
oracle pronounced it   the words stick   it is not
possible   but the god predicted   the god
threatened me with my father's bedchamber   my

mother's bed fouled desecrated   the god predicted
it   I would marry my mother   murder my father
first   then this   who could have stayed there
waiting for it   I left the kingdom   fast   I was
terrified

the high law of nature I respected that   determined
to guard that   not trusting myself   removed
myself
I was so terrified   the most impossible disaster
it seemed already to have happened   but the fear
came with me   my shadow   into this kingdom to
this throne   and it grew   till now it surrounds
me   fear   I stand in it   like a blind man in
darkness

even now   what is fate preparing for me   surely I
see that   how could I be mistaken   this plague
slaughtering everything that lives no matter what
men trees flies no matter   it spares me   why
what final disaster is it saving me for

the whole nation guttering   the last dregs of its life
no order left   ugly horrible deaths in every doorway
every path wherever you look funeral after funeral
endless terror and sobbing and in the middle of it all I
stand here   untouched   the man marked down by

the god   for the worst fate of all   a man hated
and accused by the god   still unsentenced

our lungs scorch   we gulp for breath but there's no
air the heat never moves   the sun presses down on
us with its whole strength   the dog star the lion one
on top of the other a double madness every day closer
water has left us   the old river courses crack hard
greenness has left us grass bleaches and roasts it
powders underfoot   the corn should be ripe the
harvest stands but ruined shriveled in the ear blasted
on the dry straws   the river Dirce our strong swift
Dirce it has been sealed off   springs dried up   a
bed of hot stones   infernal   a string of stinking
puddles   what light there is stifles   under this
strange fog this hellish strange reek   thickening and
hanging   all day and all night the funeral pyres are
smoldering   stench of carcasses burning   worse
stench of unburied carcasses rotting   the stars
cannot pierce through to us   the moon crawls
through this fog too close hardly visible   heaven's
cut off we're buried away here between our walls
nothing can escape the plague it fastens on everybody
young old   men women children no distinction
young men in their strength old diseased men fathers
newborn sons the plague heaps everybody together

friend and enemy man and wife burn in the one flame
nobody weeps   there are no tears left   the groans
are for the living not the dead   screaming is not
mourning but torment or terror many die of terror
leap screaming from windows gulp down poison stab
themselves for terror   fathers with roasting eyes
stoke their son's bodies in the flames mothers stagger
to and fro like madwomen between their children's
beds and the flames finally throw themselves into the
flames   mourners fall down beside the pyres and
are thrown into the same flames   survivors fight for
fuel   even snatching burning sticks from pyres
even throw their own families on top of other people's
fires   it's enough if the bones are scorched   there
isn't wood enough to turn everything to ashes   there
isn't ground enough to bury what's left   and prayers
are useless   medicine is useless   nurse and doctor
go into the flames   every hand that's stretched out
to help   the plague grips it

you high gods   I am kneeling here at your altar
beseeching you   give me death   let me go   you
great powers you decide what happens to men
listen to me   don't make me go on living in this
don't keep me here alive to watch every living thing in
my country die before I die

you are too far off and too deaf   listen to me   you
have put too much on to me   am I the only one
you're not going to let die   you are heaping death
on to everybody I am asking for death   are you
going to refuse me   have you set me apart for
something else

Oedipus   get out of this land get away from these
cries this unending funeral   this air you've poisoned
with the curse you drag everywhere   get away
run   as you should have done   long ago   run
yes even back to your parents

JOCASTA: Oedipus   you are the man we rely on you are the
King the strength   if we have strength

the heavier the threat the stronger we should find you
to bear the threat   for every challenge an answer
a king cannot sit wringing his hands reproaching the
gods   weeping like a baby   wanting to die

OEDIPUS: I have proved my courage often enough

JOCASTA: that was yesterday   it is no use to us   today we
need it

OEDIPUS: the plague is more than enough for any king   but
something beneath it   something under the roots of
it   is worse   and for me alone

JOCASTA: the dead are burning and rotting   the living are
dying   in agony   in terror   this is your people
what could be worse

OEDIPUS: the cause is worse

JOCASTA: a king's fear is a nation's fear   how can it be for you
alone   this is a new riddle Oedipus

OEDIPUS: and what if the answer is our final disaster

JOCASTA: when I carried my sons
I carried them for death   I carried them for the
throne
I carried them for final disaster   when I carried my
first son
did I know what was coming   did I know
what ropes of blood were twisting together what *
bloody footprints
were hurrying together in my body
did I know what past and unfinished reckonings

22

were getting flesh again inside me
did I think that the debts of the past
were settled before I conceived
I knew the thing in my womb was going to have to
    pay for the whole past
I knew the future was waiting for him like a greedy
    god a maneater in a cave
was going to ask for everything   happiness strength
    and finally life
as if no other man existed   I carried him for this
for pain and for fear
for hard sharp metal   for the cruelty of other men
    and his own cruelty
I carried him for disease
for rottenness and dropping to pieces
I carried him for death bones dust   I knew
but I carried him not only for this I carried him to be
    king of this
and my blood didn't pause
didn't hesitate in my womb
considering the futility
it didn't falter reckoning the odds   it poured on
into him   blood from my toes my finger ends
blind blood   blood from my gums and eyelids
blood from the roots of my hair   blood from before
    any time began

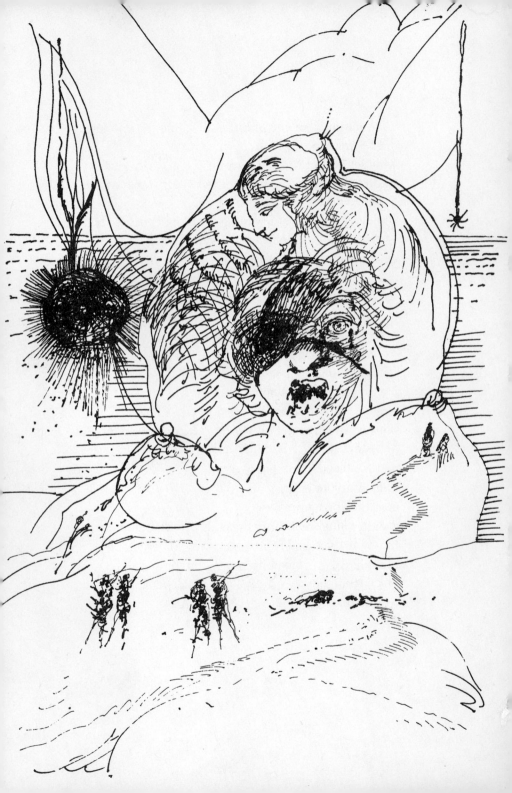

it flowed into the knot of his bowels, into the knot of
    his muscles
the knot of his brain
my womb tied everything together every corner of the
    earth and the heavens
and every trickle of the dead past
twisted it all into shape inside me
what was he   what wasn't he
the question was unasked
and what was I   what caldron was I
what doorway was I   what cave mouth
what spread my legs and lifted my knees
was he squeezing to hide
was I running to escape
the strength of the whole earth
pushed him through my body and out
it split me open and I saw the blood jump out after him
was I myself   but what was he
a bag of blood   a bag of death
a screaming mouth
was it asking a question
he was a king's son   he was a man's shape
he was perfect

not something monstrous some repulsive accident of
    wrong limbs and jumbled organs

not some freakish half-living blood clot
his eyes were perfect   feet perfect   fingers perfect
he lay there in the huge darkness like a new bright
   weapon
he was the warrant of the gods
he was their latest attempt
to walk on the earth and to live
he only had to live

and what if at that moment after all that
a doubt had turned him back

OEDIPUS: have I turned back   whatever there is that frightens
men in this world   whatever shape terror pain and
death can come in   it cannot turn me back   not
even Fate frightens me   not even the sphynx
twisting me up in her twisted words she did not
frighten me   she straddled her rock   her nest of
smashed skulls and bones   her face was a gulf her
gaze paralyzed her victims   she jerked her wings up
that tail whipping and writhing   she lashed herself
bunched herself   convulsed   started to tremble
jaws clashing together biting the air   yet I stood
there   and I asked for the riddle   I was calm
her talons gouged splinters up off the rock   saliva
poured from her fangs   she screamed   her whole

26

body shuddering   the words came slowly   the
riddle   that monster's justice   which was a death
sentence   a trap of forked meanings a noose of
knotted words   yet I took it   I undid it   I
solved it

that was the time to die   all this frenzy now   this
praying for death it's too late   Oedipus

JOCASTA: you wear the crown which was your prize for killing
that bird woman   the scepter's your prize

OEDIPUS: yet she's not dead   as if I'd never solved her riddle
she never died   she changed   I drove her off the
rock and the questions stopped   but her rottenness
is flying   her stench is a fog smothering us   as if
we were living inside her carcass

there's one hope left   the oracle   can the god direct
us

CHORUS: Thebes   you are finished
the countryside around is empty   the farmers all
dead   the workers all dead   their children all
dead   the plague owns everything

what's happened to your armies   Thebes   all
those brave men of yours   they've gone under the

plague   they're finished   they marched so
bravely away out   eastward   past the last frontiers
victory after victory   right away on to the world's
rim   leaned their banners against the sun's very
face   the conquerors   where are they?
everybody ran from them   the rich nations of the
rivers   the marksmen of the hills   the horsemen
everybody ran   towns empty   scattered   but
not any more Thebes   where are your armies now
Thebes   they're finished   the plague touched
them and they vanished   finished   rubbished into
earth

look at the streets   what are the crowds doing
black procession   they're going to the graves and the
fires   Thebes is a funeral   Thebes is choking
with corpses   why don't the crowds move   there
are too many corpses   graves can't be dug fast
enough   fire can't burn corpses fast enough   the
earth's glutted   death's glutted   and the piles of
corpses rot

the plague began with the sheep   it began with the
grass   the grass was suddenly poison   the air was
suddenly stench

a bull at the altar   massive animal   the priest had
hoisted his ax steadied his aim   in that second

before the ax fell   the bull was down   was it
touched by the god   it was touched by the plague

I saw a heifer slaughtered   her body was a sackful
of filthy tar   filthy bubbling tar

everywhere cattle are dead in the fields   dead in
their stalls   on silent farms there are bones in
cloaks   skulls on pillows   every ditch stinks
death   the heat stinks   the silence stinks

a horseman coming breakneck past us   but the
plague caught him up   it caught his horse   mid-
stride   head over heels   full tilt   down
the rider beneath it

everything green has withered   the hills that
were cool with forest   they're dusty ridges
deserts of brittle sticks   the vine's tendril is white
it crumbles when you touch it
where are the gods   the gods hate us   the gods
have run away   the gods have hidden in holes
the gods are dead of the plague   they rot and stink
too

there never were any gods   there's only death

there's something wrong with the sun   the light
seems to bulge and waver as if it were a skin ready to

split and tear   death has sickened   it's spewing its
dead up   sobbing in empty rooms   whisperings
in walls   I met myself in my own doorway
there's only death

last night the earth shook   it turned like a man
waking   it heaved like deep water in a harbor
the wells filled with blood   in the mountains cliffs
dropped away   I saw my own dead body in the
gutter

Thebes is a land of death

a death worse than death   limbs suddenly go numb
head begins to pound   your face flushes   puffs
and swells   you go into a stupor   eyes come
bulging out   ears are ringing   the gangrenous
lumps come up   every lump stabs and burns
it's a fire lit on your belly   a fire under your midriff
clots of blood come into your mouth   strings of
black blood dangle from your nostrils   you pitch
from wall to wall   coughs shatter you   burning
anything to be cooled   hug stones   fling yourself
in the river pools   crowds are at every altar
crowds shivering and groaning   crying for death
praying for death   shouting for death

ACT TWO

OEDIPUS: who is this coming so hurriedly toward the palace
is it Creon   no sight can be trusted

CHORUS: it is Creon   this is the man we are waiting for
has he brought the answer

OEDIPUS: now I shall know my fate for what it is   Creon
brother to the Queen   tell us   can the oracle
help us   what is its answer

CREON: the god at Delphi does not speak simply   as he
reveals he conceals

OEDIPUS: help hidden from us is no help   what is the god's
answer

CREON: difficult to fathom   a tangle   a riddle

OEDIPUS: tell us what it is   if it's a riddle it is for Oedipus

31

CREON: this is what the god says   the murder of King
Laius must be atoned for   the murderer must be
banished   King Laius must be avenged   not until
then shall we see the sun clear and the air pure and the
plague finished

OEDIPUS: who was the King's murderer   his throne is my
throne and his Queen my Queen   it is for me to
ask   who murdered King Laius   whom does the
god name   he will pay the penalty

CREON: if it is safe   if the god will let me   I will tell
what happened   what I went through there at
Delphi   it has altered me   I did not know what
terror was I feel it now as I speak

you know the shrine   you know the rites   I did
everything prescribed   I prepared myself purified
and humbled my thoughts   I stepped into the
shrine reverently   my hands raised in supplication
to the god

as I did so the air and the mountain shook and the
two peaks of Parnassus rumbled   like anger
avalanches of snow muttered   the mountain had
stirred   there was a silence   then the god's grove
of laurel trees trembled   drew a deep sudden breath
a hiss of leaves   from one end to the other   the

sacred spring Castalia died back among its wet stones
the priestess of the god was going ahead of me   she
began to undo her hair   and toss it loose
suddenly she was writhing from head to foot lashing
her hair this way and that   it was the god twisting
inside her   before she could reach the cave there
came a glare and a crack   I thought it was a
thunderbolt directly upon us louder than a man can
imagine   but it was a voice
    Good stars shall come again to the Thebes of
      Cadmus
    only when that runaway regicide
    known to the god now and from infancy
    no longer pollutes Dirce the lovely river
    murderer you crept back into your mother's
      benighted womb

OEDIPUS: it is a warning from the god   the burial honors for
the dead King's remains   they were neglected
the succession was left open   scepter unclaimed
the throne empty   for any usurper   I am going
to do now what you failed to do then   kings must
protect kingship   this man   you all feared him
he dies   he's forgotten

CREON: we did not forget   terror stupefied us

34

OEDIPUS: what terror could prevent you mourning a king

CREON: terror of the sphynx   and her threats   her riddle
stupefied us

OEDIPUS: the movers the guides the lawgivers   are above
they are demanding expiation for this murder
vengeance for Laius   the King of Thebes
where is the man

you great gods   you who choose kings from among
men and set them up and keep them in power
come down and hear these words   you who made
this whole universe and the laws we have to live and
die in   hear me   and you   great burning
watcher   who look after the seasons of this earth
who give sap and blood its strength   who pace out
the centuries   and you who govern darkness   and
you   muscle of the earth   who move and speak
in the winds and in water   and you who manage the
dead   be with me now   hear these words I
speak   now

let no walls hold peace for the man whose hands killed
King Laius   wherever he goes let him be luckless
unprotected   hounded by every evil   let his
genius desert him   let every land reject him   let

35

him marry in shame   let his children be born in
shame   let his bed be a torture   a pit and a
rack of shame   and let him deal as bloodily with his
own father   as he dealt with Laius   let him
suffer to the last   wrench everything   and nothing
could be worse than this   everything that I have
escaped   for that man forgiveness no longer exists

by the power of the sea   you who guard my
homeland on every side   by you highest god of the
lightbeams you voice of the oracle   by the
kingdom which I now rule   by the gods of the home
I left   I make an oath   let my father live to
enjoy his old age and his throne in peace   let my
mother never marry any other husband   only as I
dig out this criminal only as I tear the full penalty out
of his living body   only as I avenge Laius

tell it again   where did the murder happen   how
did it happen   open combat   treachery   tell it

CREON: the King was going to Delphi   to the oracle   a
hard road   broken country   at a certain point the
road forks   three ways lay before Laius

he expected a pleasant journey   through friendly
people   but there   at the crossroads   in the

thick of the scrub forest bandits met him an
awkward place trapped between the dense thickets
nobody saw the fight

just as we need him here is Tiresias the oracle's
roused him

OEDIPUS: Tiresias the god's chosen mouth explain the
words of the oracle they seem to demand the life
of a man name him

TIRESIAS: if I am slow to speak Oedipus if I ask for time
be patient a blind man misses much the god's
servant my country's servant I am here to
search this thing to the bottom when I was young
when my blood was hot the god came down into me
into my body he spoke directly out of my mouth in
his own words we must look at the omens
bring to the altars a pure white bull also a heifer
that has never been yoked

MANTO: they are here

TIRESIAS: I need more help yet you must guide me my
daughter in this too as we sacrifice these beasts you
describe the signs describe every token to me

MANTO: the victims are perfect and prepared

TIRESIAS: now recite the prayers   summon the holy presences
burn the incense

MANTO: I have piled the incense on the hearth of the altar

TIRESIAS: Now describe the flames   you have fed the fire
but does it eat

MANTO: it flared up   tall and fierce   then suddenly died
back   to nothing

TIRESIAS: did the flame stand up clear   what was its color
did it point cleanly straight up   like a blade   or
was it broken   crooked in any way   was it ragged
or smoky in any way   describe it

MANTO: it changed   it was every color together all twisting
together   a full rainbow but clouded   not easy
to say what was not there   dark and purplish to
begin with   flecked with yellows   it reached up
and shook turning red   till it was all blood red
suddenly it blackened and guttered   now   look

TIRESIAS: describe everything

MANTO: the flame is climbing up again   it's splitting into
two horns   splitting from itself   father the wine
we poured for the libations it is blood it's become blood
the altar fire is belching black smoke   oily heavy
smoke   what does it mean   the smoke is reaching
out toward the King   it is looping and thickening
round the King's head   it's blotted the King's face out
now it spreads   it's spreading over everything
covering everything hanging   blackish   a canopy
not moving   it's made a gloom   what does it
mean

TIRESIAS: voices   fighting voices   voice against voice
voices are tearing me   voices but not words
nothing is steady   whirling   impossible to hold
this is something terrible   something hidden
when the gods are enraged they speak out clearly you
hear them clearly   but now they cannot speak
they are trying to drag into the light something too
horrible for the light   something they are ashamed
of   what is it
quickly offer them the animals   put the salt meal on
their necks   are they calm   how do they take
you touching them   describe everything

MANTO: the bull tosses his head he's frightened he seems afraid
of the sun he keeps wheeling his head away from the
sun he's shining with sweat and shivering

TIRESIAS: do they go down at the first stroke

MANTO: the heifer surged with her whole weight against the
blade   a single stab and she's down   not the bull
the bull's lurching about   the sword's gone in twice
up to the full depth   but he's still staggering
trying to get away   he's down   he heaves
shudders a little   now he's still

TIRESIAS: what about the blood   tell about the blood   does
the blood spout from the wounds   or does it ooze
reluctant to come out

MANTO: the heifer's blood is coming in a river   the bull's
wounds are as big but they're bloodless   they're just
holes ripped in the red meat   instead blood's
bursting from his eyes and out of his mouth   black
lumpy torrents of it   his blood is black

TIRESIAS: this sacrifice is evil   my whole body freezes as I
listen to you   but go deeper lift out the entrails
describe all that you see

MANTO: something is wrong   no membrane to contain the
entrails and the intestines quake   father what can
this mean   usually they quiver a little but these are
twisting   shuddering look how they shake my arm
as if they had separate life   much seems to be
missing   much of the intestines   the heart is
missing no here is the heart shriveled withered up
diseased black buried down here far from its natural
position what does it mean father   everything is
reversed   the lungs are squeezed here far over to
the right gorged with blood how did they breathe
the liver is rotten breaks in my hand oozing black
bitter gall   look   this liver is double headed
the left wing swollen twice its proper size knotted with
great veins   the right wing is deathly white fungus
rotten but the finger of it is enormous stiff black with
blood   that is a fatal omen

every position is wrong how did nature survive in this
what is this thick lump here deep down here father
horrible   a fetus   an unborn calf   this heifer
was never mated but here is a calf   and how did the
womb get here   the calf's kicking inside the bag
jerking for life   it's groaning inside the bag blood is
everywhere
the bull is getting up   and the heifer   a dis-

emboweled carcass is getting up on to its legs   it
lunges at the priests   hooks with its horns entrails
dragging after it   that noise is the fire   that
bellowing is the altar fire   the altar itself is
bellowing

JOCASTA: what does this sacrifice mean   what is hidden under
all this

OEDIPUS: speak plainly to me Tiresias   my ear is not afraid of
the truth whatever it is   when the worst is certain
men become calm

TIRESIAS: you shall live to envy this torment Oedipus

OEDIPUS: the gods are trying to make me understand one thing
tell me that one thing   who murdered King Laius

TIRESIAS: birds deep in the sky   organs pulled bleeding alive
from deep in the bodies of animals   how can such
things spell out a name   for the name Oedipus we
need other methods   for the name we need the dead
King himself   Laius himself dead beneath the earth
he must be brought back   out of that darkness
Laius must name the murderer himself   we must

open the earth have talk with death open the ears
of the dead open their mouths   Oedipus   who
performs this   it cannot be yourself   a king's
eyes are for this world   they must be kept well clear
of the fouling shadows of that other world

OEDIPUS: Creon   second in line to the throne   this is for
you

TIRESIAS: while we reach into death and call out the dead let the
men sing   let them sing against the dead

Chorus to Bacchus

OOO-AI-EE . . . KA

CHANT   3 times

REPLY   3 times

DANCE DEATH INTO ITS HOLE

DANCE DEATH INTO ITS HOLE

INTO ITS HOLE

ITS HOLE

ITS HOLE

ITS HOLE

HOLE

LET IT CLIMB
LET IT COME UP
LET IT COME UP
LET IT CLIMB
LET IT LIVE
OPEN THE GATE
OPEN THE GATE
LET IT LIVE
TEAR THE BLOOD
OPEN ITS MOUTH
LET IT CRY

WHILE THE WIND
CROSSES THE STONES

WHILE THE STARS TURN
WHILE THE MOON TURNS
WHILE THE SEA TURNS

WHILE THE SUN STANDS AT THE DOORWAY
YOU   YOU   YOU
YOU UNDER THE   YOU UNDER THE
YOU   UNDER THE LEAF
YOU   UNDER THE STONE
YOU   UNDER BLOOD   UNDER THE SEA   } 2 times
YOU   UNDER THE EARTH

UNDER THE LEAF
UNDER THE STONE
UNDER BLOOD   } repeat
UNDER THE SEA
UNDER THE EARTH

YOU   YOU   YOU   YOU
YOU   YOU   YOU   YOU

UNDER BLOOD
UNDER THE EARTH

YOU

ACT THREE

OEDIPUS: in your face Creon I see only horror   whose life do
the gods demand from us   this whole city is
waiting to hear you

CREON: you want me to speak   fear forbids me to speak

OEDIPUS: when Thebes is down this royal house your own house
is down   I command you to speak

CREON: you command me to speak   you will pray you were
deaf

OEDIPUS: ignorance cures nothing   this whole nation is sick
speak   you can cure it

CREON: the cure can be so drastic   men prefer the sickness

OEDIPUS: when torture has crushed you   will you fear the
anger of the crown   when will you speak

CREON: crowns have been crushed by the words of the tortured

OEDIPUS: you shall go back to the underworld   in your own
blood like the cattle a cheap sacrifice   unless you
tell us what these rites have revealed

CREON: a king cannot grant a man less than his silence

OEDIPUS: the silence in a kingdom can be deadlier than the speech

CREON: if silence is forbidden   freedom is finished

OEDIPUS: power to command finished   the throne is finished
the kingdom finished

CREON: prepare yourself Oedipus

at the source of the river Dirce   in a narrow valley
is a clump of black hollies   in the thick of it a
gigantic cypress   reaching out over the whole wood
a huge shadow imprisoning everything   an oak tree
ancient and massive   has died there   laurels
myrtles and alders   all struggling for the light   but
the place belongs to the cypress   right in among its
roots a spring wells up   freezingly cold   it is

49

almost dark in there   underfoot quagmire   a
stinking slime

as soon as the old priest arrived he started   he didn't
need to wait for the night in that gloom   they dug a
trench   into that they threw burning wood brought
from the funeral pyres   the priest begins to make
movements with sprays broken from the cypress   to
and fro   black robe trailing behind   twisted yew
twigs round his head and white hair   black sheep
and black oxen are dragged backward and toppled
alive into the burning trench   the bellowing does not
last long   flames leap up   smoke and the stench of
burning flesh fill the wood

now the priest begins to call up the things of the
underworld   he calls to death itself over and over
working himself into an ecstasy   face contorted foam
thickening around his mouth   he argues with the
dead   he cajoles and threatens   screams mutters
sings whispers   and now more blood on to the altars
more living animals into the flames   the trench
swamped with new blood   milk too   and wine
poured from his left hand   and that incantation over
and over   bowed to the ground   stamping
voice convulsed not human any more   bringing the
dead up   then we felt the ground shaking   we felt

the earth lift under us and the wood shook   suddenly
dogs were baying   a hellish yelling of dogs   it was
shaking the earth   coming up   and Tiresias was
shouting "they have heard   I have opened death
they are coming" twigs and dust rained down   great
trees split from top to bottom and lifted their roots as
the earth began to tear open

I saw things in the darkness   moving   many pale
masks lifted and sinking   I saw dark rivers and
marshes   I saw writhing things

I could hear human voices and the screeching and
laughing of mouths that were never on earth   I heard
sobbing deeper than anything on earth

I saw every disease I knew their faces I heard them
and knew their voices   I saw every torment every
injury every horror spinning like flames and shadows
sickening forms faces mouths   reaching up clutching
toward us and crying

I saw the plague of this city   bloated   blood
oozing from every orifice   grinning up   on a
sliding mountain of corpses

the roaring of dogs' voices screams jabbering groans
indescribable laughter   erupting   as if the earth
were crammed splitting with it   Manto is accus-

tomed to the old man's miracles but she stood petrified
too   none of us could move   only Tiresias seemed
in control of himself   but he could see none of it
he carried straight on   he began to call for the ghosts

and they came   a growing sound   a humming
that seemed to silence everything   like a vast flock of
autumn starlings a rushing gloomy wind of twitterings
beating up at the light   swirling back and round and
round in the pit   grabbing at the earth the tree
roots at our clothes   all crying in their thin bodiless
voices   till at last one of them laid hold of the roots
and clung there   his face pressed into the earth
Tiresias called to this creature commanding it to come
up   again and again he called   and at last it looked
up   it lifted its face and I recognized   Laius
our King   Laius   he pulled himself up   it was
him   his whole body was plastered with blood   his
hair beard face   all one terrible wound   a mash of
mud brains blood   his mouth lay open and the
tongue inside it began to move and quiver   he began
to speak
     you insane family of Cadmus
     you will never stop slaughtering each other
     finish it now   rip your children with your own
        hands put an end to your blood now
     because worse is coming

an evil too detestable to name is squatting on the
   throne of Thebes
my country rots   but it isn't the gods
it is this   a son and a mother
knotted and twisted together   a son and a mother
a couple of vipers, bodies twisting together
blood flowing back together in the one sewer
it isn't the wind   fevers from the south or your
dried out earth   the drought and its scorching dust
those things are innocent
it is your King
blinded in the wrong that got him his throne   blinded
to his own origins   blind to the fixed gods   the
loathed son of that same Queen who now swells under
him   the Queen   yes   worse than him   the
Queen   and her womb that chamber of hell
which began it all   he pushed his way back there
where he began   worse than an animal   he buried
his head in there   there where he first came
screaming out   and brought new brothers for himself
out of his own mother's body   horrible tentacles
of evil   a bloodier tangle than his own sphynx

you   clutching that scepter which does not belong
to you   I am the man you murdered for it   your
father   still not avenged   but I'll bring a brides-

maid to your marriage   a fury to bind you and
your mother together with a whiplash   I shall
disembowel your city   I shall start your sons
butchering each other   I shall rip your whole infernal
lineage out by the roots   men of Thebes   get rid
of this monster   drive him away   no matter where
only let him go quickly   let him take that deadly
shadow of his elsewhere   then your streams will
recover   and the roots will revive and blossom come
again and the fruit swell   a pure air will sweep
through the land   and the grief the pestilence the
death pains the horror the death   they will all follow
his footsteps

he'll want to get away fast   but I shall stop him   I
shall block his path   and shackle his feet   I shall
break his heart   he'll go away from you groping
over darkened roads   suddenly an old man

Thebes   take the earth from him   his father will
take the light

OEDIPUS: the thing I most dreaded in this world   I'm accused
of having done it   this thing I've run from and
hidden from and guarded myself against   the thought
of it horror of it with me every second   dreading to

55

OEDIPUS: what you haven't yet got

CREON: convicted without defense

OEDIPUS: who defended me   yet I stand here convicted   you
urge me to go   who rules when I go

CREON: what if I am innocent

OEDIPUS: this man is guilty   take him to the prison in the
rock   guard him

CHORUS

The gods hate Thebes   the gods are punishing this city
they have always detested us   they will not spare Thebes

Cadmus began it
Cadmus
killed a god's serpent

he sowed its fangs in a plowed field
what jumped out of the furrows
an army of madmen   a maniac army
they started butchering each other
fresh out of the earth   started a massacre
butchered each other over their mother's body
and that was the beginning of this noble city   which the gods
hate

the gods sent Oedipus to Thebes
Oedipus was their answer
dragging the plague as he dragged his foot
now he comes under the curse of Thebes
like Actaeon before him   the hunter
who looked too close at the wrong woman
peered through the leaves at the forbidden body
of the woman in the pool
Actaeon's own hounds turned against him
as the gods have turned against us
they turned against him   deaf to his voice   their eyes had
changed
and he ran from the yelling of his own hounds
he ran as a dumb stag
driven like a stag in a circle
sick with the terrors of a stag
bowels emptying and heartbroken
lungs torn and blood in his mouth
till he saw in that same pool he was a stag
and he was dragged down as a stag
torn to pieces as a stag
in a ring of his own blood-covered hounds
the pool where the woman had lifted her thigh was a wallow of
blood
a black hole of hounds rending

Oedipus has come under the curse of Thebes

ACT FOUR

OEDIPUS: Before   it was fear   but now   is it certainty
    how have I been trapped
I killed Laius
the voice of the oracle accuses me
his own ghost points at me and accuses me
but my conscience   acquits me
I know myself
better than any ghost   better than the god at
    Delphi knows me
Laius is nowhere in my conscience

Laius murdered   if I could remember something
if I could go back
two men only   two strangers   both together
long ago
I see it   I see myself shoved to the roadside
shoved into the thorns
the horses driven straight at me   to trample me
to go over me with the wheels
the lathered horses   that arrogant screaming old
    man

and the driver shouting
trying to run me down with the chariot
it was one half self-defense what I did
I put my spear into the driver   and he fell out
   backwards
as the chariot passed the old man slashed at me
with his sword
I drove the spear through him and he fell between
   the horses
they ran on and dragged him tangled in the reins
   under the chariot
it was all done in a moment   as they passed me
a long time ago   a long way away   at a
   crossroads

JOCASTA: Oedipus   leave the dead alone   stop these
   diggings into the past   bringing my dead husband
   back to show his wounds and show himself still in
   death agony   leave him alone   hell cannot be
   opened safely   what can come out of it   only
   more pain and more misfortune   more confusion
   and more death

OEDIPUS: Jocasta   tell me this   when Laius died
   how old was he

JOCASTA: at the end of middle age

OEDIPUS: on that last ride how many rode with him

JOCASTA: many set out   but the roads to Delphi are broken
the country difficult   and Laius was a hard
traveler

OEDIPUS: how many stayed with him

JOCASTA: he outstripped them all   he went ahead alone

OEDIPUS: the King was alone

JOCASTA: when he arrived at the crossroads he was alone
with the driver of his chariot

OEDIPUS: the driver was also killed

JOCASTA: the driver fell there at the crossroads   the horses
dragged the body of Laius on toward Delphi
nobody saw the fight   so they were found

OEDIPUS: there is no escaping this   I know who saw that

fight   when did it happen

66

JOCASTA: let it lie Oedipus   it happened   no man can
alter what has happened   I make no secret of it
to you   that death was waiting for Laius   fate
only adjusted the balance when he fell to the earth
he owed me a life   I bore him a boy and before
my milk had entered its mouth he snatched it away
things I have never spoken   a crime I shall not
dig up were tangled in those reins that dragged his
dead body away from the crossroads   a man of
stone broken by stones   forget him Oedipus
finish with riddles   forget the oracle
burrowing in that darkness cannot save us   only
strength can save us

OEDIPUS: when was Laius killed   how long ago

JOCASTA: this is the tenth summer

(*Enter* MESSENGER.)

MESSENGER: the men of Corinth call you to your father's throne
Polybus has gone to his last rest

OEDIPUS: how did my father die

MESSENGER: asleep   smiling   in peace

OEDIPUS: my father is dead   without hurt   from any
man   no murder   witness   my hands   I
can raise them to the light   innocent   my hands
cannot be accused   but something is left   the
worse half of my destiny   the half I fear most
that still remains

MESSENGER: in your father's kingdom you need fear nothing

OEDIPUS: only one thing keeps me from running toward it
with all my strength

MESSENGER: what is that Oedipus

OEDIPUS: my mother

MESSENGER: your mother   why fear her   she is longing for
you to come now   quickly

OEDIPUS: her love is what I fear

MESSENGER: can you leave her a widow

OEDIPUS: those words go too deep

MESSENGER: who is tormenting you   what is your secret

tell me   kings have trusted me before   even
with their greatest secrets

OEDIPUS: long ago the oracle told me this   I shall marry my
mother

MESSENGER: then you can forget the oracle   this fear is unreal
your speculations are empty   Merope was never
your mother

OEDIPUS: why should the King of Corinth adopt a stranger

MESSENGER: an heir to the throne forestalls many troubles

OEDIPUS: who shared such a secret with you

MESSENGER: it was these hands   these very hands   when you
were a whimpering baby   these   handed you
to Merope

OEDIPUS: you gave me to my mother   then where did I
begin   who gave me to you

MESSENGER: a shepherd   on Mount Cithaeron

OEDIPUS: how did you come to be on that mountain

Mount Cithaeron   iron was twisted through his
ankles   you were meant to expose him on the
mountain   for the wild beasts   I see your face
change   you are searching for words too carefully

PHORBAS: you are digging too deep

OEDIPUS: the truth is as it is   let it come out as it is

PHORBAS: it is all too long ago

OEDIPUS: speak or I shall torture you till you speak

PHORBAS: on a day long ago   yes   I handed this man a
crippled baby boy   it was hopeless we were too
late   it could never have lived

OEDIPUS: why could it never have lived

PHORBAS: the iron through its feet   those cruel wires
that knot of filthy iron   the wound was putrid
it stank   the whole body festering   burning

OEDIPUS: it's enough   my fate has found me at last   who
was this child   who was it

PHORBAS: I swore never to speak

OEDIPUS: I shall burn that oath out of you

PHORBAS: will you destroy a man for one little fact

OEDIPUS: I am not a madman   you only need to speak
who was that child   you are the only man who
knows   who was its father   who was its mother

PHORBAS: its mother

OEDIPUS: who was its mother

PHORBAS: its mother was your wife

OEDIPUS: birth   birthbed   blood   take this   open
the earth bury it   bottom of the darkness
under everything   I am not fit for the light
Thebans your stones   now put a mountain on
me   hack me to pieces   pile the plague fires
on me   make me ashes   finish me   put me
where I know nothing   I am the plague   I am
the monster Creon saw in hell   I am the cancer
at the roots of this city   and in your blood and in
the air   I should have died in the womb

suffocated   inside there   drowned in my
mother's blood   come out dead   that first day
before anything   Oedipus wait   now I need
that strength   something to fit this error   drag
up the root of it   and out   something for me
alone   first I shall go to the palace   quickly to
seek out my mother   and present her with her son
my mother

CHORUS

If only our fate were ours to choose   you would see me on
quiet waters   where the airs are gentle   a full sail but a
light wind   no more than a breath   easy voyage   that is
best   no blast no smashed rigging no flogging downwind into
cliffs   under surge   nothing recovered   no vanishing in
mid ocean

give me a quiet voyage   neither under cliffs nor too far out
on the black water where the depth opens   the middle course
is the safe one   the only life   easily on   to a calm end
surrounded by gains

foolish Icarus   he thought he could fly
it was a dream
tried to crawl across the stars
loaded with his crazy dream   his crazy paraphernalia
the wings the wax and the feathers

78

up and up and up
saw eagles beneath him   saw his enormous shadow on the
   clouds beneath him
met the sun face to face
fell

his father Daedalus was wiser   he flew lower
he kept under clouds   in the shadow of the clouds
the same crazy equipment   but the dream different
till Icarus dropped past him   out of the belly of a cloud
past him
down
through emptiness
a cry   dwindling
a splash
tiny in the middle of the vast sea

ACT FIVE

CHORUS: who is that   it is one of the King's slaves   beating
        his head with his fists   something has happened
        what has happened   tell us

SLAVE: When Oedipus grasped his fate   and saw the full
       depth of wrong where he had lost himself   he
       understood the oracle   now he's condemned himself

       he hurried straight back to the palace
       his stride was savage and heavy   like a beast
          purposeful
       never paused
       went in under that terrible roof

       face deathly   he was groaning   muttering
       he was a crazed beast   a wounded lion
       that's going to die killing
       his eyes bulged   demented   blazing with all that
          torment inside him
       mad grimaces kept wrenching his face

sweat poured on his temples and neck
froth stood round his mouth
his hands kept gripping at his stomach
he was trying to tear himself open
to gouge out the bowels and liver and heart the whole
  mass of agony
he was toiling for something
some action something unthinkable
something to answer all that has happened
he began to shout   why delay it
I should be stabbed   smashed under a rock
I should be burned alive   there should be animals
ripping me to pieces
tigers eagles ripping me with their hooks
Cithaeron   you mountain
you began it all   it's your slopes should have had
  my carcass
your wild dogs should have cracked my riddles for me
where are your wolves
and that woman who wrenched her husband's head off
  on your lovely grass
wrenched it off and ran with it   send her   Agave

why be afraid of death it's nothing am I afraid
death   it's only death
can keep a man innocent

then he pulled out his sword and he was going to kill
    himself
but he stopped he began to reason
one little jab of pain   a few seconds of death in my
    eyes and in my mouth
can that pay for a lifetime like mine
can one stroke cut all my debts off
one death   that's for your father   that's good
but what about your mother
and what about that doubled blood in your children
what about their shame
what about Thebes   all the dead   all those living
    with their deaths on them
they are doing your penance for you Oedipus
and you cannot pay you cannot possibly pay
not in this lifetime
you need to be born again   suffer for everything
    again
and die again   over and over   lifetime after
    lifetime
every lifetime a new sentence
and length of penalties
think   death can come only once
think   this death has to last   has to be slow
find a death
find a death that can still feel

and go on feeling   a life in death   a death among
     the living
why are you hesitating Oedipus

suddenly he began to weep   everything that had been
torment suddenly it was sobbing   it shook his whole
body and he shouted   is weeping all I can give
can't my eyes give any more   let them go with their
tears   let them go   eyeballs too   everything
out   is this enough for you you frozen gods of
marriage   is it sufficient   are my eyes enough

he was raging as he spoke   his face throbbed dark
red   his eyeballs seemed to be jumping in their
sockets   forced out from the skull   his face was
no longer the face of Oedipus   contorted   like a
rabid dog   he had begun to scream   a bellowing
animal   anger   agony tearing his throat

his fingers had stabbed deep into his eyesockets   he
hooked them gripping the eyeballs   and he tugged
twisting and dragging with all his strength   till they
gave way   and he flung them from him   his
fingers dug back into his sockets he could not stop
he was gibbering and moaning insane with his fury
against himself   gouging   scrabbling with his
nails

in those huge holes in his face
the terrors of the light are finished for Oedipus
he lifted his face   with its raw horrible gaps
he tested the darkness
there were rags of flesh strings and nerve ends
still trailing over his cheeks   he fumbled for them
snapping them off   every last shred
then he let out a roar   half screamed
you gods
now will you stop torturing my country
I've found the murderer   and look   I've punished
    him
I've forced him to pay the debt
and his marriage   I've found the darkness for it
I've found it the night it deserves
as he was screaming his face seemed to blacken suddenly
the blood vessels had burst inside his torn eyepits
the blood came spewing out over his face and beard
in a moment he was drenched

CHORUS

Fate is the master of everything   it is vain to fight against fate
from the beginning to the end the road is laid down   human
scheming is futile   worries are futile   prayers are futile

sometimes a man wins   sometimes he loses
who decides whether he loses or wins
it has all been decided long ago elsewhere
it is destiny
not a single man can alter it
all he can do is let it happen

the good luck the bad luck everything that happens
everything that seems to toss our days up and down
it is all there from the first moment
it is all there   tangled in the knotted mesh of causes
helpless to change itself
even the great god lies there entangled
helpless in the mesh of causes
and the last day lies there tangled with the first
a man's life is a pattern on the floor   like a maze
it is all fixed   he wanders in the pattern
no prayer can alter it
or help him to escape it   nothing

then fear can be the end of him
a man's fear of his fate is often his fate
leaping to avoid it   he meets it

OEDIPUS: all is well   I have corrected all the mistakes and
my father has been paid what he was owed   I like
this darkness   I wonder which god it is that I've

86

finally pleased   which of them has forgiven me for all
that I did   he's given me this dark veil for my head
pleasant
the light   that awful eye   that never let me rest
and followed me everywhere   peering through every
crack   at last you've escaped it   you haven't driven
it away   you haven't killed that as   you killed your
father   it's abandoned you   left you to yourself
simply   it's left you to your new face   the true face
of Oedipus

CHORUS: Look   Jocasta coming out of the palace   demented
look at Jocasta   why has she stopped   look at her
she's staring at her son   she hardly knows what's
happening   darkness is nearly swamping her
there he stands   blasted   his blind mask turned to
the sky   she wants to speak   she's afraid of him
she comes closer her grief stronger than everything
she's stepping toward him

JOCASTA: what can I call you now   what shall I call you
you're my son shall I call you my son
are you ashamed
you are my son   I lost you
you're alive   I've found you
speak to me

show me your face
turn your head toward me show me your face

OEDIPUS: you are making all my pains useless   you are spoiling
my comfortable darkness   forcing me to see again
go away   we must not meet   the salt bottomless
ocean should be washing between our bodies   not to
cleanse them nothing can cleanse them   if another
world hangs somewhere   under some other sun
and lost away among other stars   one of us should be
there

JOCASTA: you were my husband   you are my son   you
killed my husband   I bore your sons   nothing
can be blamed   everything that has happened is here
there is no road away from it

OEDIPUS: no more words mother   I beg you by all that in our
names is right and wrong   let there be no more words
between us two

JOCASTA: nothing in me moves   can I not feel   I shared the
wrong   how do I share the punishment   it's me
I'm at the root of it   I am the root   my blood is
the dark twisted root   this womb   darkness
swallowing all order and distinction   so die   let

out this hell that lives in you   nothing would be
enough to punish it   if god smashed his whole
universe on to me it wouldn't be enough   a mother
a morass   all I want is death   find it   you
killed your father   finish it   the same hand
your mother   finish it   is this the sword that
killed him   is this it that killed my husband and my
husband's father with a single stab   where shall I
have the second stab   this point under my breast
or this long edge across my throat   don't you know
the place   it's here   this   the place the gods
hate   where everything began the son the husband
up here

CHORUS: look   her hand slackens from the hilt   the whelm
of blood squeezes the blade out

OEDIPUS: you god of the oracle   you deceived me lied to me it
has not turned out as you said   only my father's
death was required it was enough   it has been
doubled and the blame has been doubled   my mother
is dead and her death comes from me   both my
father and my mother are dead under my fate   it is
more than I was promised   now go   the dark
road   quickly   quickly begin   do not stumble
on the body of your mother   you people of Thebes

crushed under this plague your spirits broken look   I
am going away   I am taking my curse off you
now you can hope again   lift your faces   now you
will see the skies alter   and the sun and the grass
everything will change now   all you stretched out
hoping only for death your faces pressed to your graves
look up   if you can move now   if you can breathe
suck in this new air   it will cure all the sickness
go and bury your dead now without fear   because
the contagion is leaving your land I am taking it with
me   I am taking it away   fate   remorseless
my enemy   you are the friend I choose   come with
me
pestilence   ulcerous agony   blasting consumption
plague terror   plague blackness   despair
welcome   come with me   you are my guides
lead me

(The CHORUS celebrate the departure of OEDIPUS with a
dance)

MESSENGER: with my flock   I was also a shepherd

OEDIPUS: there's a strange mark on my body   what do you
know about it

MESSENGER: sharp iron hooked through your heels   to cripple
and hobble you   you were meant to die
the wounds were infected and swollen   and so
you are called Oedipus   that scar must be still on
your feet

OEDIPUS: who gave me to you   tell me that

JOSCASTA: listen to my warning Oedipus   the dead man will
never be satisfied   not until you are dead and
under the ground with him   the dead hate the
living   they only want to murder the living
turn your eyes toward the living   give your
strength to us   darkness is too deep you will
never see to the bottom of it   the dead will rob
you of everything

CHORUS: listen to the Queen Oedipus

OEDIPUS: who gave me to you

MESSENGER: the master of the King's flocks

OEDIPUS: what was the man's name

MESSENGER: I am old   that was long ago   it has been too
long buried

OEDIPUS: his face   could you recognize that

MESSENGER: perhaps

OEDIPUS: call in the shepherds   let them drive all their
beasts to the altars   bring the head shepherds
bring them to me here

JOCASTA: Oedipus   listen to your wife

CHORUS: listen to her Oedipus

JOCASTA: the truth is not human it has no mercy why rush
into the mouth of it   you have a kingdom to
protect

OEDIPUS: I am enmeshed in a mystery worse than any death

CHORUS: you want to satisfy yourself   but your people will
have to pay   your Queen will have to pay   it is
not chance that hides these things and keeps them

72

hidden   leave things as they are   let fate unfold
at its leisure   do not force it

OEDIPUS: if it were endurable I would endure it   why do
you all warn me back   what is the truth

CHORUS: you were born to the throne   isn't that enough
don't look any deeper Oedipus

OEDIPUS: what blood am I   I shall find it out   whatever
it means   here is Phorbas   this ancient man
was once master of the King's flocks   do you
remember the name   Phorbas   do you
remember the face

MESSENGER: the man is familiar   I have seen that face before
in the days of King Laius did your flocks graze
Mount Cithaeron

PHORBAS: the rich grass of lovely Cithaeron   that was our
summer pasture   we were there every summer

MESSENGER: do you recognize me

OEDIPUS: do you remember a baby a boy   that you handed
to this man   one day long ago on the slope of